DOTTO AND THE
MINOTAUR'S MAZE

ALKIS ALKIVIADES & GIOVANNI CASELLI

HARRY N. ABRAMS, INC., PUBLISHERS

ISBN 0-8109-2778-0

Published in 1998 by Harry N. Abrams, Incorporated, New York

 Harry N. Abrams, Inc.
100 Fifth Avenue
New York, N.Y. 10011
www.abramsbooks.com

Conceived, edited and designed by
Dotto International Limited, London

Editor, Kate Petty
Computer artwork, Anthony Duke
Production, Charles James
Origination by Fotographics Ltd., London & Hong Kong

How to Play

This is an interactive dot-puzzle adventure book.
You will need dice and a re-particalizer (a pencil) to play.
In this game you move from page to page as directed
by the puzzles, **not** in numerical order.

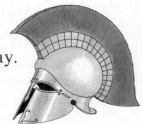

Your Mission

In the comic strip on pages 8 and 9 you will see that the Evil Eraser has appeared on a Cretan island in ancient Greece to unleash the Minotaur and other horrible mythical creatures. A plea for help arrives in Professor Delius' laboratory. It comes from Princess Ariadne, who has been particalized by the Eraser.

Dotto's mission is to find and defeat the Minotaur, imprison it, and restore Ariadne. To defeat the Minotaur, Dotto must collect six magic items (a **Shield**, a **Sword**, a **Spear**, a **Helmet**, a **Breastplate**, and **Greaves**) that have been scattered around the maze-like island. It is your job to help him by connecting the dots to re-particalize the objects and people that have been erased.

The point of the game is to survive all the challenges you meet on the way and collect the six items that will point the way to the location of the Minotaur, so you can defeat it, and restore the beautiful Ariadne, thus foiling the Evil Eraser.

What to Do

There are 18 Locations. After reading the comic strip, choose a starting point for Dotto to land on the island, complete that dot puzzle, and go to the Location number that is revealed. Choose **only one** dot puzzle to complete. Some Locations may contain two or three puzzles, each in a different color. The first dot in each puzzle is a white 1 in a solid-colored circle and the last dot is in a box. When you connect the last dot, the number of a Location will be revealed. Go to that Location and continue until you reach the final one. Be prepared to meet lots of challenges along the way!

Challenges

The dot puzzle you choose might also include one of the six items Dotto needs to defeat the Minotaur. Each time you complete a puzzle that includes one of these items, match it to the one on the Adventure Panel on page 5 and put a check in the box below it. Then, each time you reach the Armory at Location 3, find the weapon/armor you have collected and complete the dot puzzle around that item. By the time you have done all six puzzles, you will have discovered all the items Dotto needs to track down the Minotaur, vanquish it, and complete his mission.

Battles

Beware the Evil Eraser's beasts, the legendary and mythical creatures of evil! You will recognize them by the EE badge: ✖. If you choose to fight an evil creature, you must first arm yourself with a **golden thread charm**, then throw the dice to see whether you win (2,4,6) or lose (1,3,5) the battle. If you win, you can complete the dot puzzle and proceed. If you lose, you can try again with another charm. Ariadne has given Dotto ten charms to start off with. Put an x on each charm in the Adventure Panel on page 4 as you use it. You might also discover **spare charms** in other Locations during the adventure. Some are included in the puzzle, others are free. Put check marks on the spare charms in the Adventure Panel as you collect them and cross them out as you use them. If you run out of charms, you can try to collect some more before fighting another creature. However, if you reach a point where you have to fight a creature in order to move on and you have no charms, you must leave the game. Remember, you'll need at least three charms to defeat the Minotaur at the end of the adventure!

Getting Knocked Out of the Game

Beware! The Evil Eraser has set traps on the island. You could be struck by lightning, kicked by a wild horse, or worse! If this happens, you are thrown off the island into the vectoral void and must start again. You do not need to redo any finished puzzles or fight any previously defeated creatures.

Choices

You can choose only one dot puzzle to complete before moving to another Location. Sometimes, you will see a number before you complete a dot puzzle, either because you have already connected the dots or because it is a "free" Location. You can choose to go through one of these doors without completing any puzzles in that particular Location if you prefer.

Adventure Panel

Golden Thread Charms

This is your personal store of charms. These magical items ward off evil and help guide you on the right path. You will need one for protection before you can do battle with one of the Evil Eraser's creatures (you will recognize the creature by its ✄ badge). Put an x in the circle under each charm as you use it.

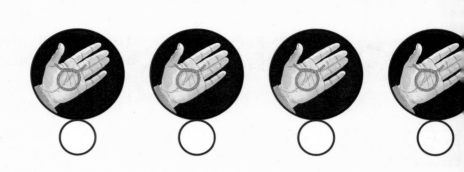

Spare Golden Thread Charms

There are spare charms to be picked up as you make your way from one Location to another. When you find a spare charm put a check below one here and add it to your stockpile. Turn the check into an x when you use the charm. Remember that if you lose a fight with one of the Evil Eraser's creatures, you will need to use another charm to fight again.

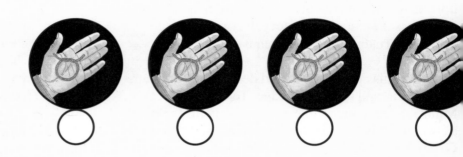

Armor and Weapons

Dotto cannot locate and fight the Minotaur until he has armed himself with six magic items of warfare. These are: a Shield, a Helmet, a Spear, a Breastplate, a Sword, and a pair of Greaves. You will discover these items as you move from Location to Location. Whenever you find one, turn back to this Adventure Panel, put a check in the box next to the corresponding item, and label it. Each time you end up at Location 3 (the Armory), check this page to see which new items you have found, and complete the puzzle nearest that item.

Only when you have found all six pieces of armor and completed all six puzzles will you see the number of the secret Location. Then you will be able to fight the Minotaur, rescue Ariadne, and finish the adventure.

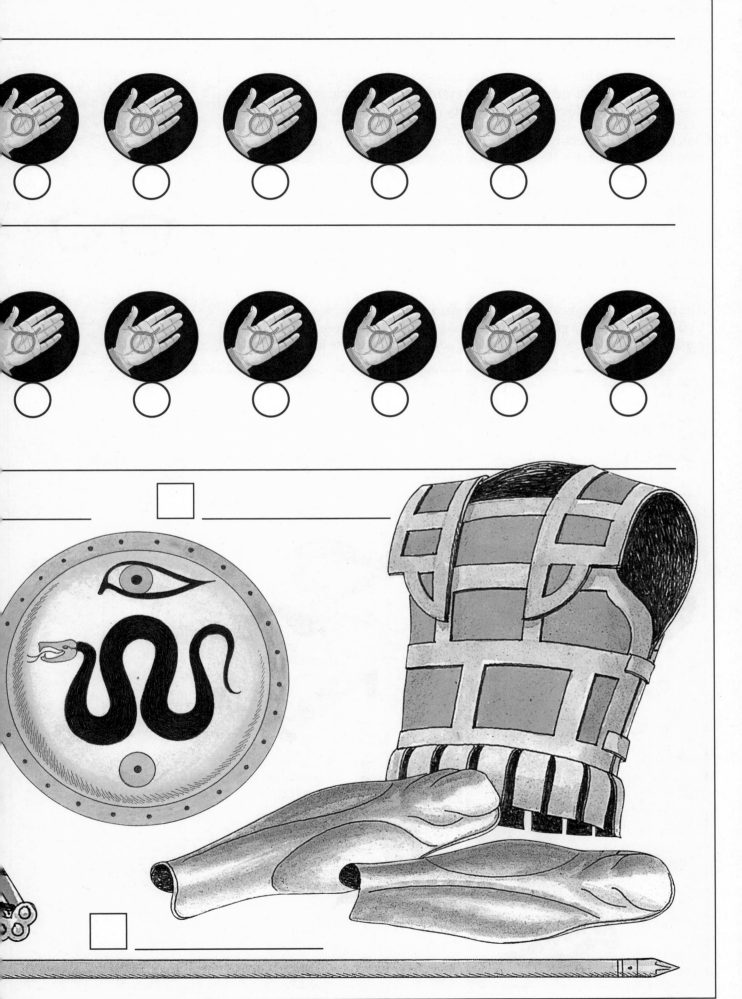

The story so far...

Professor Delius is a scientific genius. Many years ago he was awakened in the middle of the night by the sound of an explosion in his laboratory. When he went to investigate, there was no sign of an intruder, but to his dismay, his latest invention, a new particle accelerator, was in pieces. For a long time the mystery remained unsolved.

After months of detective work the professor eventually discovered the identity of the intruder. He was an ex-employee, another scientist who wanted to steal the plans for the particle accelerator and pass them on to a rival company. Although the thief escaped from the laboratory without a scratch, the explosion had warped his mind. He had seen enough to build a particalizer for himself, one that would reduce people and things to mere dots. He called himself the Evil Eraser and set off on a bizarre career of crime. Ever more twisted and daring, the Eraser enjoys causing chaos wherever he goes in time and space.

The professor has dedicated his life to repairing the damage caused by the Evil Eraser. He built a portable re-particalizer that could restore anything particalized by the Eraser and trained his nephew Dotto to use it.

Professor Delius
The inventor of the time-vortex particle accelerator and a famous scientist, Delius has set up a Time-Space alarm system that tells him when and where the Eraser has struck. The system also has a video

THE EVIL ERASER

This is one of the few existing pictures of the Eraser. It shows him wearing a mask to cover his disfigured face. The masks the Eraser wears are believed to be his power source. This mask will fall from his face when Dotto successfully completes his mission, forcing the Eraser to retreat to his own time to think up new dastardly deeds.

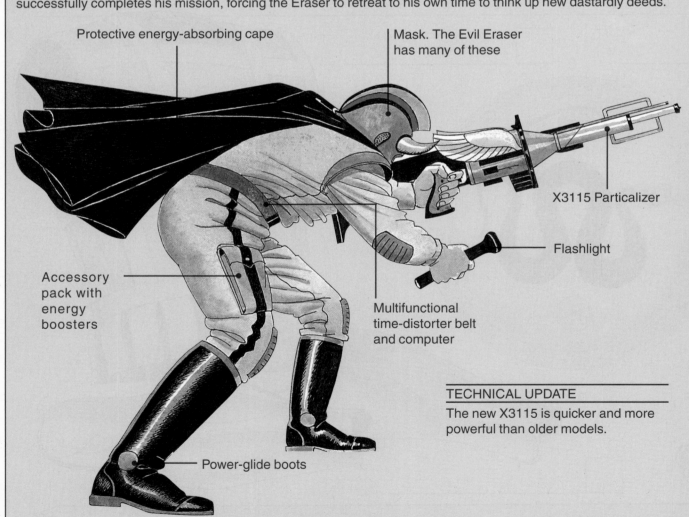

Protective energy-absorbing cape

Mask. The Evil Eraser has many of these

X3115 Particalizer

Flashlight

Accessory pack with energy boosters

Multifunctional time-distorter belt and computer

Power-glide boots

TECHNICAL UPDATE
The new X3115 is quicker and more powerful than older models.

link that provides pictures of the events as they are happening. It is even capable of picking up small objects and beaming them back to the laboratory.

Pursuing the Eraser
Delius can tune into events caused by the Eraser's particalizer but once particle warfare breaks out he still needs to have someone "in the field" - wherever in time or space this happens to be. When Dotto is on a mission he maintains contact with the professor through his Dattcom headset.

Dattcom Headset

Time-Space tracking sensor

Visor with mini-screen

Communicator/Receiver unit linked to the professor's laboratory

Flashlight

Particle sensor

New lightweight re-particalizer

TECHNICAL UPDATE

Dotto's new suit is lighter and more comfortable, while his new re-particalizer is technologically more advanced than the old model. The new Dattcom Headset is a vast improvement on Dotto's old, heavy accessory pack.

Shock absorbers on knees

DOTTO

Needing someone young and healthy to fight for him, the professor recruited his nephew, Dotto. Now Dotto pursues the Evil Eraser through time and space to restore objects and people that have been turned to dots. Unfortunately, if Dotto re-particalizes a deadly beast, he must fight it.

Although the Evil Eraser has experience and possibly a technical advantage on his side, Dotto is younger and in better shape and has the protection and wisdom of his uncle behind him.

Multisurface grip boots

NOW READ ON!

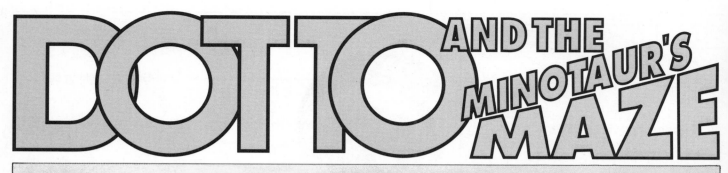

DOTTO AND THE MINOTAUR'S MAZE

DOTTO IS WORKING OUT IN HIS BIO-GYM, STAYING IN SHAPE. HE NEVER KNOWS WHEN HE WILL BE NEEDED...

IN HIS LABORATORY PROFESSOR DELIUS HAS FALLEN ASLEEP OVER A BOOK OF GREEK MYTHS. HIS CAT IS PURRING AND HIS TEA IS GETTING COLD. ALL IS PEACEFUL...

SUDDENLY!

ZZZZZ

BZZZ!!!!

Apion.

IT'S THE TIME SPHERE VORTEX DETECTOR - IT MUST BE THE ERASER!!

LET'S CHECK THE **SCREEN!**

HEAR ARIADNE, OH MIGHTY GODS! THE MINOTAUR IS LOOSE ON OUR ISLAND WITH OTHER BEASTS OF LEGEND! MY PEOPLE ARE STRICKEN WITH TERROR, MAY THE GODS SEND A CHAMPION TO CAPTURE THE MINOTAUR AND STOP THIS DEVASTATION!!

THE LIGHTHOUSE

THE HARBOR

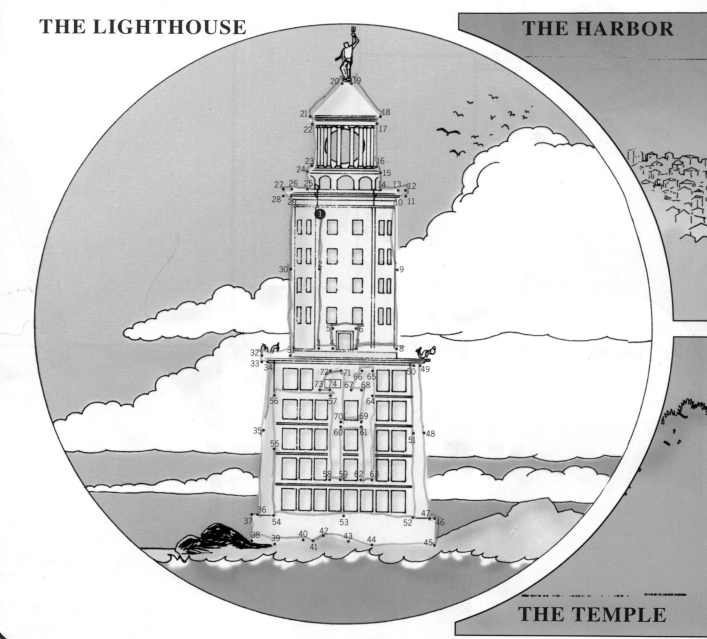

THE TEMPLE

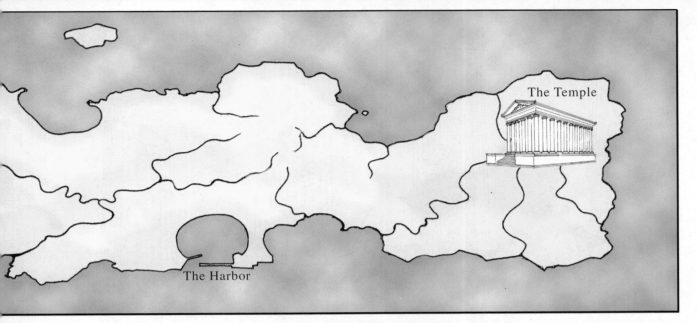

The Temple

The Harbor

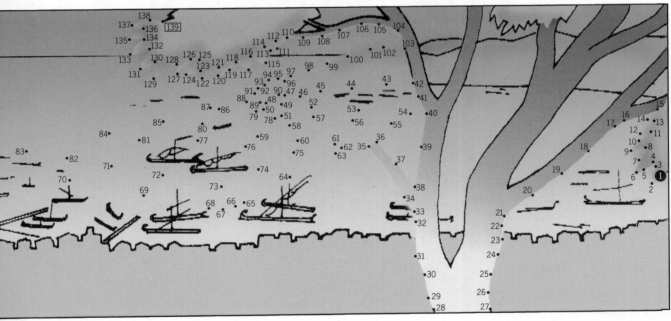

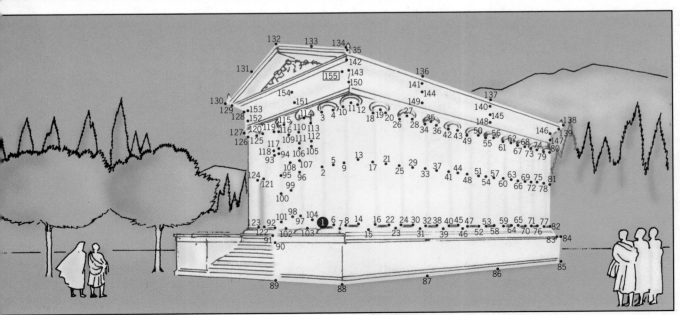

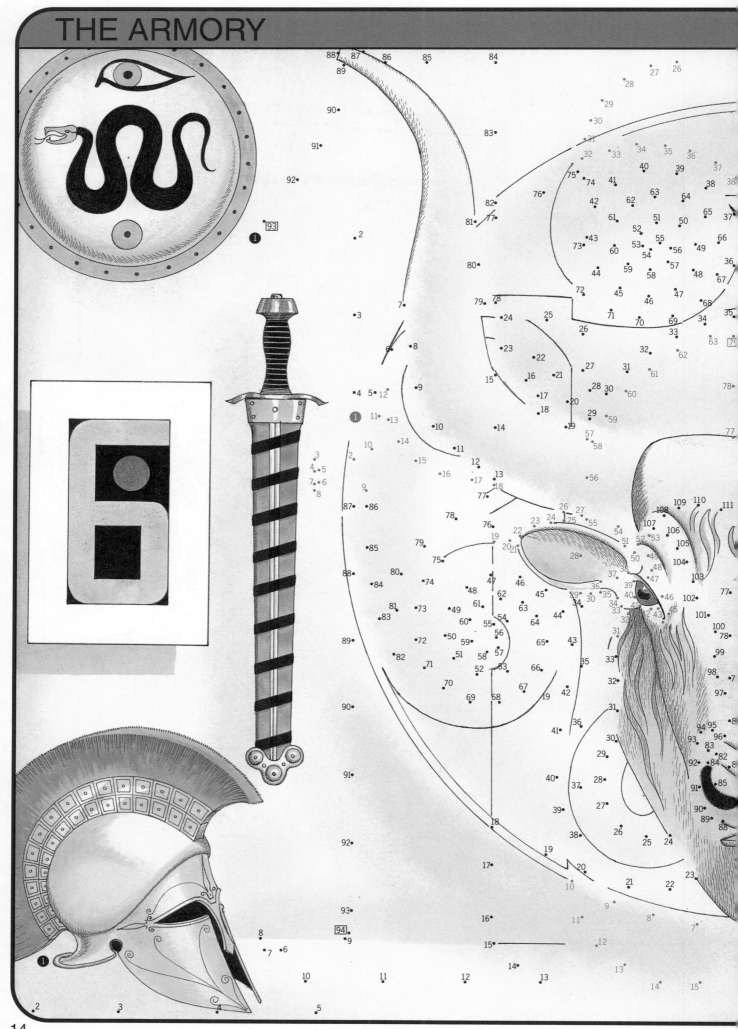

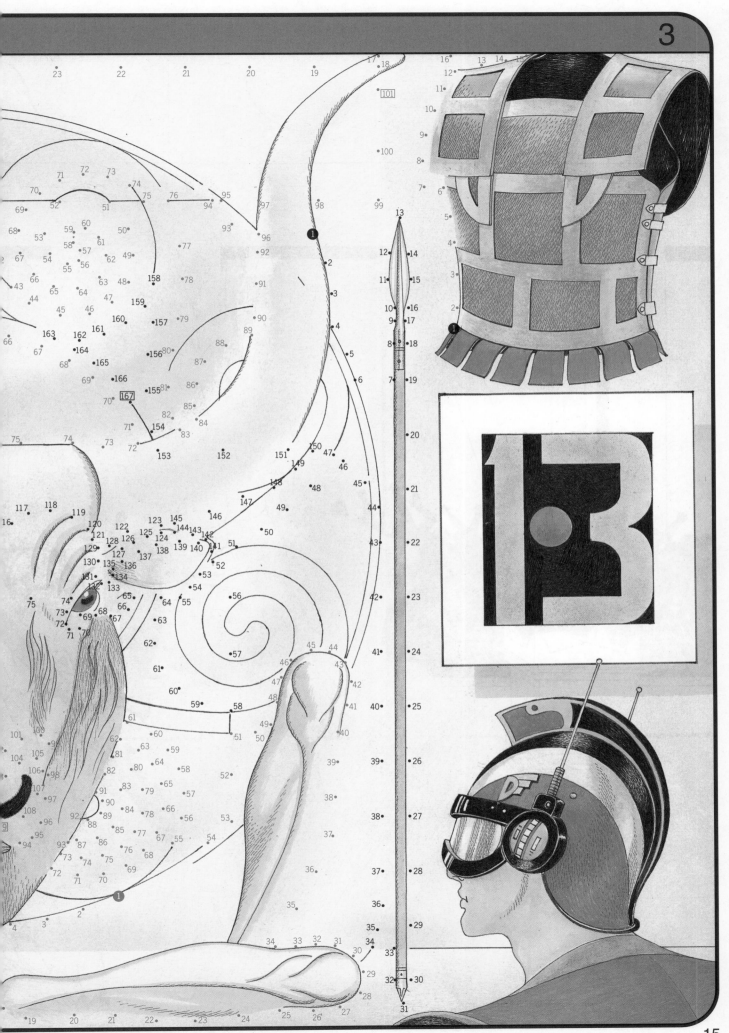

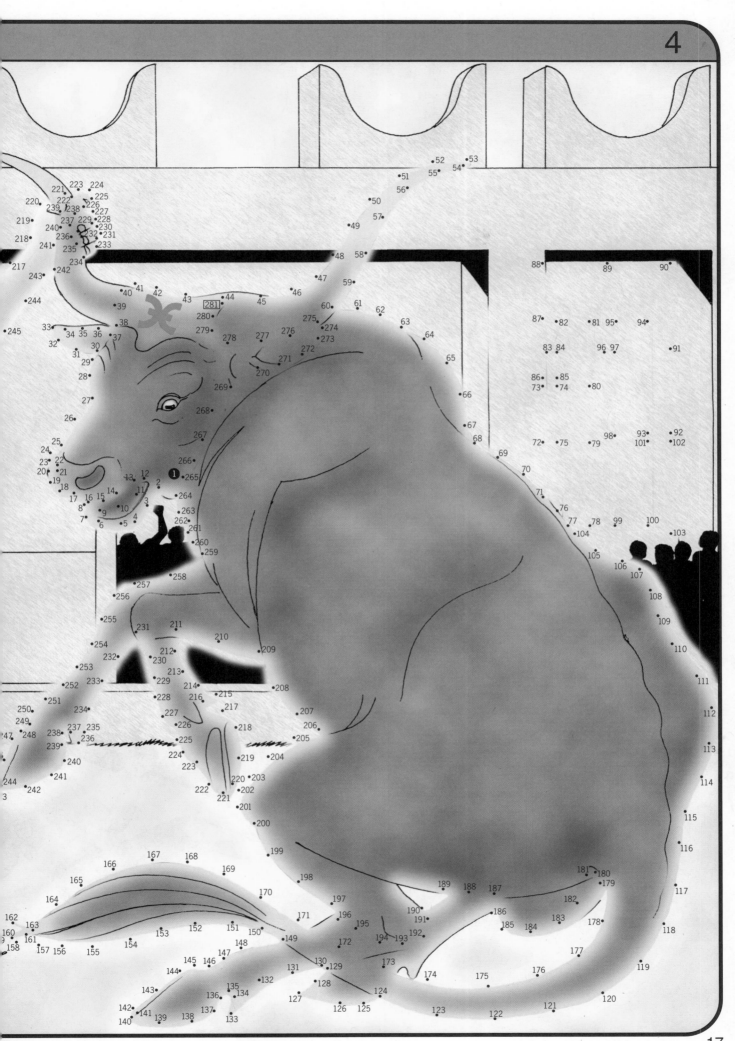

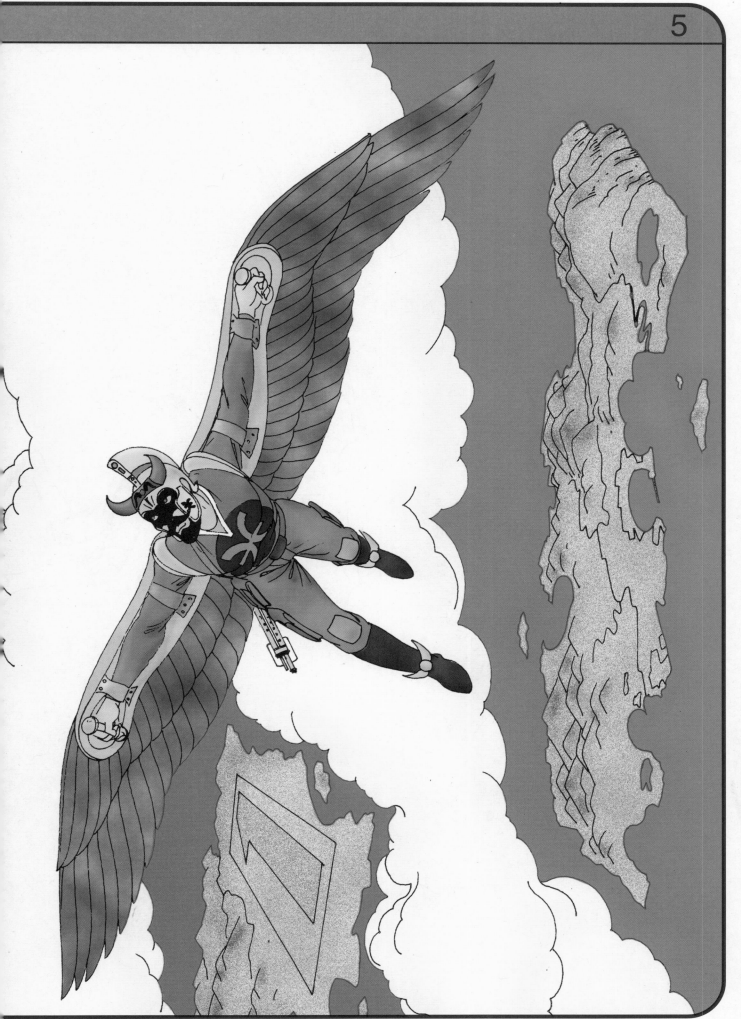

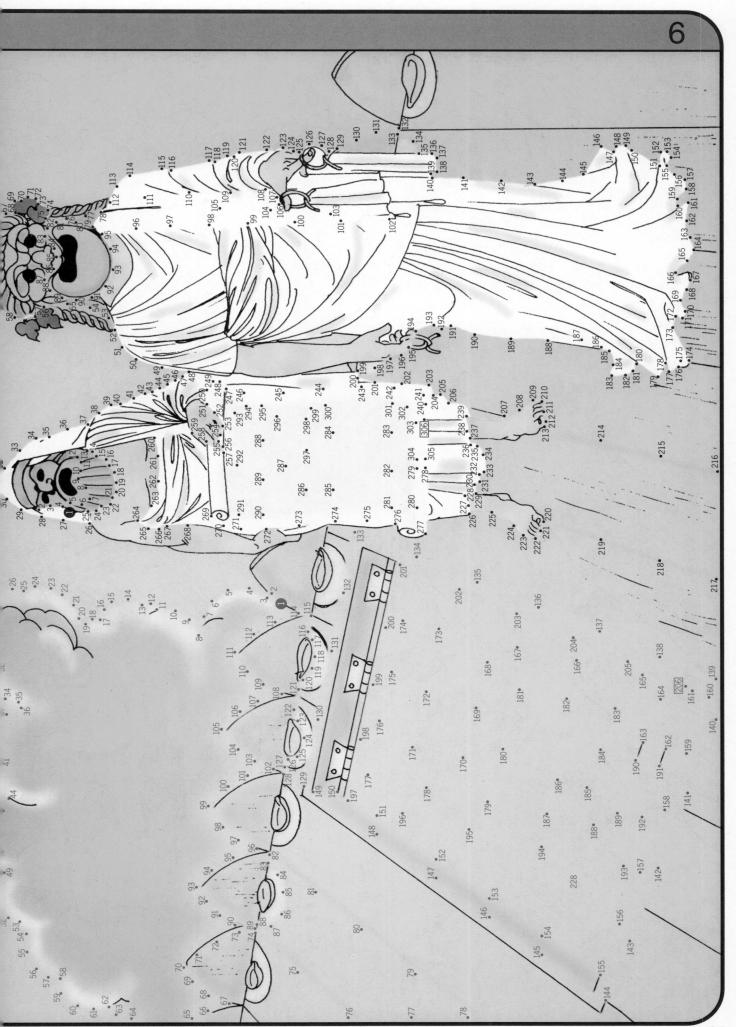

CHOOSE WISELY, DOTTO!

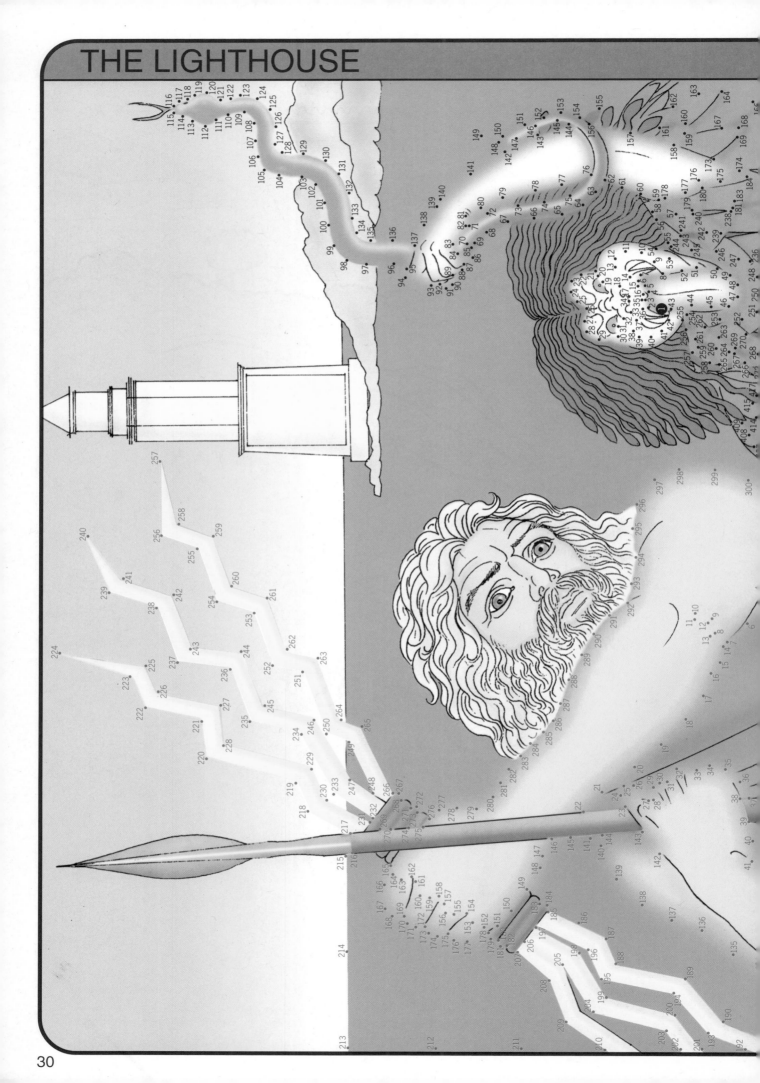

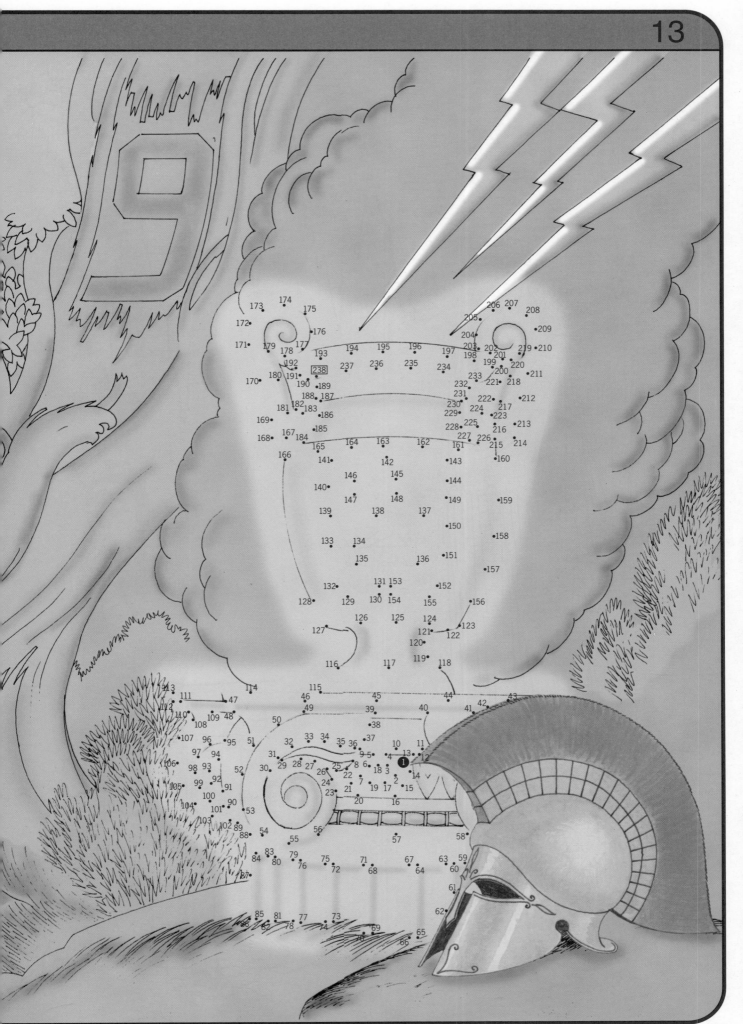

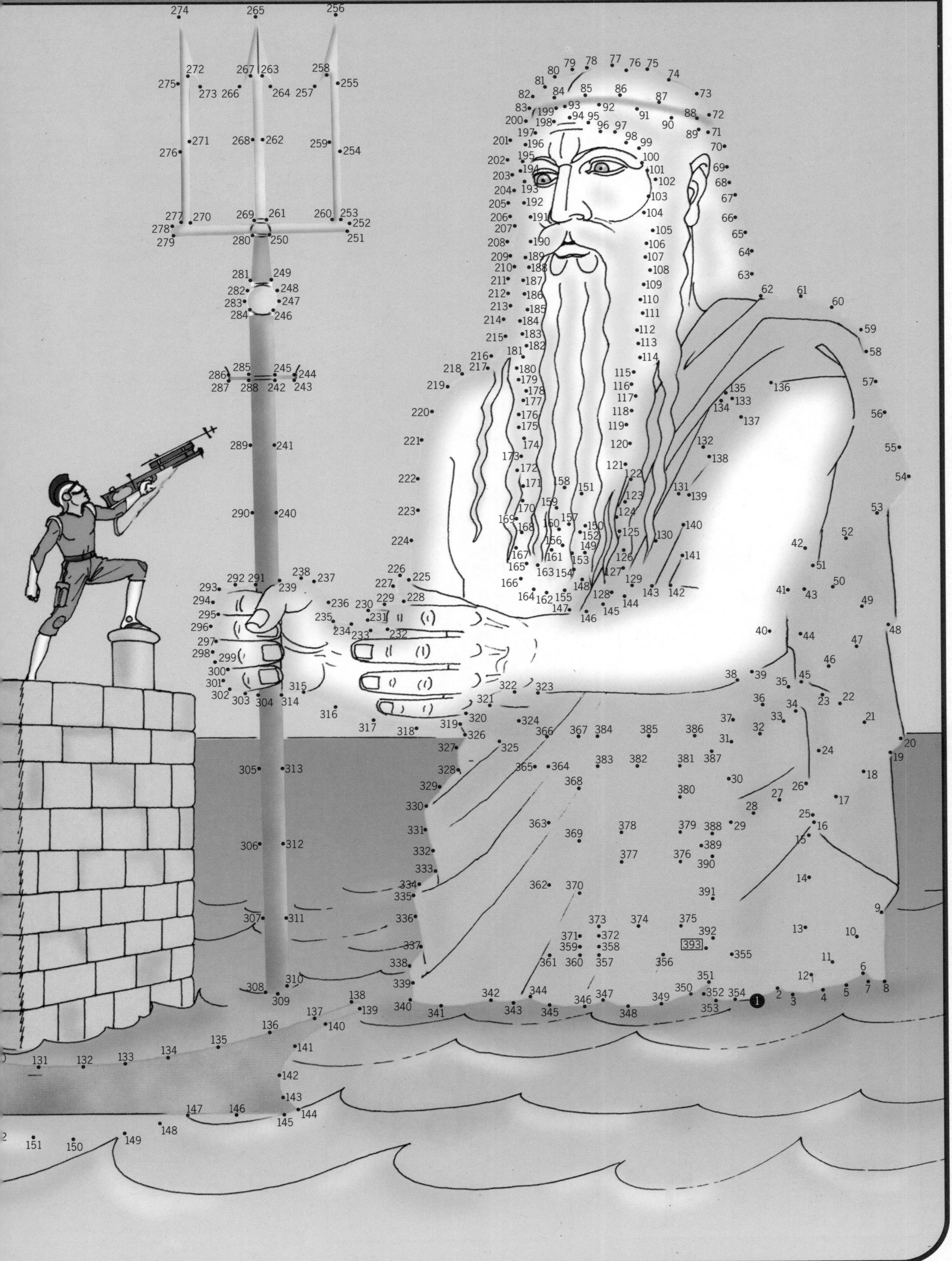

Minoan Crete

This adventure takes place on an island similar to the ancient Greek island of Crete. Crete was first settled by farmers in about 6000 BC. The present adventure is set in classical times, 1,000 years after the height of Cretan civilization, when the myth of Theseus, Ariadne, and the Minotaur was very popular in literature and the theater. By then, the Cretans had developed a strong economy, skilled craftsmen, and a number of large palaces. One of the palaces was excavated by Sir Arthur Evans in 1894. He made many discoveries, particularly in the palace called Knossos. Sir Arthur Evans called the ancient Cretan civilization "Minoan," named after Minos, a legendary Cretan king.

The Minoans were people who farmed crops such as grapes, olives, wheat, and barley. They also kept animals, hunted in the wild interior of the island and fished along its shores. The Minoan kings always had a large fleet of ships which they used for trade with other countries. Minoan pots have been found all over the eastern Mediterranean, including Egypt.

Minoan pots and burial places feature two important symbols which also appear on their palace walls. The first is the image of a bull's horns (the bull was sacred in Minoan Crete) and the second is the double-headed axe (Labrys).

The Myth of the Minotaur

All of the creatures, beasts, and gods shown in this book are based on Greek mythology. Myths are stories created to explain unusual events. The myth of the Minotaur concerns a Greek hero called Theseus who heard that his fellow Greeks were being forced to send young men and women to the island of Crete to be eaten by a horrible creature called the Minotaur. The Minotaur was half-man, half-bull and lived in a large maze called the Labyrinth that was very difficult to get out of once you were inside. Theseus joined the doomed men and women and made the journey to Crete. King Minos' daughter, the Princess Ariadne, fell in love with Theseus and, before he went into the Labyrinth, gave him a sword and a magic thread. Theseus tied one end of the thread to the entrance of the maze and went inside. He found and killed the Minotaur in a furious battle and then followed the thread back to the entrance again and into Ariadne's arms.

Bull Leaping

This was a religious ritual associated with the sacred bull and shown on palace wall paintings (called frescoes). Young men and women would form teams, then each player would try to get as close as possible to the bull as it charged across the palace courtyard. The player would then grasp the bull's horns, jump on its back, and then back onto the ground.

Bulls and Double-axes

According to legend, the Cretan King Minos was the son of Europa and the god Zeus, who himself grew up on Crete and sometimes took the form of a bull.

The bull was a prominent feature of palace decoration and the shape of the coping-stone (above right) is obviously inspired by bulls' horns. Such decorations can still be seen in the palace.

The double-axe (Labrys) is associated with Knossos and the palace of King Minos known as "the home of the double-axe" or the Labyrinth. The first palace at Knossos was built circa 2000 BC. The final one was destroyed by fire 600 years later.

The Greek vase illustrated below shows the final struggle between Theseus and the Minotaur. Daedalus, the famous artisan who built the Labyrinth, told Ariadne how to enter and leave the maze. He gave her the magic thread which she, in turn, gave to Theseus.

Find the Objects

The illustrations below show a number of mythical creatures, gods, and historical objects from ancient Greece. Can you figure out which Locations they were in? Refer to your completed dot puzzles and write the Location number in the box by the picture. You will find the answers on page 48.

1

2

3

4

5

6

7

8

9

10

11

12

Answers

1. Apollo
Location 9
Apollo was the God of the Sun, Light, and Truth. Apollo killed his mother's enemy, the serpent Python, at his shrine at Delphi. He then made Delphi the location of his "Oracle," where ordinary people could talk to him and ask questions.

2. The Charybdis
Location 7
The Charybdis was a terrible whirling phenomenon that could wreck ships and kill humans. The hero Odysseus barely managed to escape its fury.

3. The Actors' Masks
Location 6
The Western theater tradition can be traced back to ancient Greece. Each actor wore a painted mask. The expression on the mask showed the character's age, sex, and feelings. Actors could switch parts by simply putting on another mask. Large open mouths in the masks made the actors' voices louder and deeper.

4. The Medusa
Location 11
Medusa was one of the mythical monsters called Gorgons. The Gorgons were once three devastatingly beautiful sisters, but they were turned into monsters for offending the goddess Athena. Medusa had serpents for hair and anyone who looked at her turned into stone.

5. The Pythia
Location 9
The Pythia was the priestess who spoke on behalf of the god Apollo at the Oracle of Delphi. Oracles were places where you could ask the gods anything you wanted. The Pythia dressed in white and sat on a three-legged stool called a tripod, holding a branch of laurel in her hand.

6. Poseidon
Location 15
Poseidon was the brother of Zeus. The Greeks worshipped him as the ruler of the seas. He had an underwater palace where he kept a gold chariot that was pulled by white horses. Poseidon was also known as the Earth-shaker because people thought he caused earthquakes.

7. The Harpies
Location 6
The Harpies were mythical flying bird-like monsters who pestered humans by stealing their food and screeching to prevent them from sleeping. The Harpies persecuted King Phineus until Jason and the Argonauts helped get rid of them.

8. Zeus
Location 11
Zeus was the ruler of all the gods who lived on Mount Olympus and he controlled the heavens. He was married to his sister Hera but had many relationships with ordinary women whom he approached in different guises: such as a swan or a bull.

9. Pegasus
Location 12
A flying horse with shining white coat and wings, Pegasus was the offspring of Poseidon (the ruler of the seas) and Medusa (the Gorgon). He was generally placid and did what he was told. He helped a Greek hero called Bellerophon in his many adventures and carried thunderbolts for Zeus.

10. Persephone
Location 14
A goddess, the daughter of Zeus and Demeter, Persephone represented Spring and new growth. Hades, the God of the Underworld, made her his bride. But she was unhappy in the Underworld so Zeus allowed her to spend half the year away. This, the Greeks believed, is why we have Fall and Winter months and Spring and Summer months.

11. Charon
Location 14
Charon was the ferryman who, Greeks believed, took dead souls across the river Styx to the banks of the Underworld. Those souls whose relatives had provided them with a coin paid Charon to take them across the river. Those who had no coin were left to wander endlessly.

12. The Seven-Headed Hydra
Location 13
A mythical monster with a dog-like body and seven serpent heads, the Hydra caused death and destruction as it terrorized the swamps of Lerna. It was killed by the hero Hercules as one of his twelve labors. The heads of the Hydra would grow again once cut off, but Hercules solved this problem by sealing the wounds with fire.

GOOD JOB READER! IF YOU ENJOYED ADVENTURING WITH DOTTO THROUGH ANCIENT GREECE, TRY YOUR HAND AT UNLOCKING THE SECRETS OF ANCIENT EGYPT IN **DOTTO AND THE PHARAOH'S MASK!** ISBN 0-8109-2783-7